About this book

Hippos are usually placid animals, spending their days wallowing in the lakes and rivers of Africa, taking mud baths or basking on sandbanks. However, they can be vicious when roused and can inflict severe wounds with their tusks. Moreover, these amphibious mammals can cause havoc on cultivated land — crashing through crops and devouring huge quantities of young plants. C. H. Trevisick gives a full account of the day-to-day life of this so-called "river horse." He describes clearly its extraordinary mating behavior, its feeding habits and the playful antics of young hippos. He also explains how and why these animals were hunted mercilessly until their existence was endangered and they became protected by law.

About the author

Charles Trevisick is the founder and former owner of the long-established Ilfracombe Zoo Park. He broadcasts regularly on radio and television, and is the successful author of several books on various zoo animals and pets. He is a Fellow of the Zoological Society of London.

Sir Maurice Yonge, Consultant Editor to the series, is Honorary Fellow in Zoology in the University of Edinburgh.

Animals of the World

599, 73
T

First published in 1980 by
Wayland Publishers Limited
49 Lansdowne Place, Hove
East Sussex, BN3 1HF, England

Typesetting in the U.K. by Granada Graphics
Printed in Italy by G. Canale & C. S.p.A., Turin

First published in the United States of America by
Raintree Publishers Limited, 1980

Library of Congress Cataloging in Publication Data

Trevisick, Charles.
  Hippos.

   (Animals of the world)
   Includes index.
   SUMMARY: Introduces the physical characteristics,
habits, and natural environment of the hippopotamus.
     1. Hippopotamuses—Juvenile literature.
[1. Hippopotamuses] I. Title. II. Series.
QL737.U57T73 1980   599'.734   79-19672
ISBN 0-8172-1087-3 lib. bdg.

Animals of the World
Consultant Editor: Sir Maurice Yonge CBE FRS

Hippos

C. H. Trevisick

RAINTREE CHILDRENS BOOKS
Milwaukee • Toronto • Melbourne • London

Hippopotamus (hippo, for short) means "river horse," and indeed these magnificent mammals live in, and beside, the rivers and lakes of Africa. However, hippos do not look much like horses and are not related to them at all. You may be surprised to learn that they *are* distantly related to another common domestic animal — the pig!

The hippo is a heavy, bulky animal with a long, barrel-shaped body, short legs, a large, heavy head and an enormous blunt jaw. When it is standing on swampy land, its belly nearly touches the ground. It has small ears, which are rounded at the tips, and a

short, powerful neck. The hippo's great strength enables it to crash through the thick undergrowth of the African forests.

Its broad feet have four short toes. For an animal of its size it has a surprisingly short tail. There are no hairs on the hippo's body, except for the bristly hairs on its tail, inside the ears and on the snout. The skin is usually brown or gray, but it can also be gray and blue, reddish brown, or spotted. "Albino" hippos have also been found: these are a brilliant pink because the blood vessels are near the surface of the skin.

The Amphibious or Common hippopotamus is the largest land animal after the African elephant and the rhinoceros. A full-grown bull, or male, hippo can be as long as 4 m. (13 ft.) and sometimes stand 1.2 m. (4 ft.) high. It may weigh as much as four tons. The hide, or skin, of a hippo is extremely thick and heavy. It is used to make "sjamboks" (which are a kind of whip), helmets and belt buckles.

The ancestors of the hippo, which are now extinct, were once found in various parts of the world: in Palestine, around the foothills of the Himalayas, on the island of Madagascar, and throughout Europe. Remains of the Maltese hippo have been found in the rock caverns of Malta and Sicily. Fossilized remains of hippos have also been discovered in London and as far north as Yorkshire, showing that in the distant past these animals must have played in the muddy rivers and grazed on the plains of England.

Now, however, the hippo can only be found in the central parts of Africa, and in a few protected areas, such as the Kruger National Park in South Africa, and the national parks of East Africa. These carefully supervised game reserves have

4

thousands of visitors each year. Here the hippo lives in a safe environment.

Hippos were once thought to "sweat blood." We now know, however, that the hippo has no sweat glands and that the "blood" is in fact a pink, sticky substance which is discharged from pores in the skin. This secretion forms a protective coat which keeps the hippo waterproof (*left*).

The Common hippo is very much at home in the water, where it spends a great deal of its time. It can stay underwater for as long as five minutes. It can swim very fast and can also walk along the bottom of a river for

short periods. The ears and nostrils can be closed so that water does not enter when the hippo dives. The eyes and nostrils are set on top of the hippo's head. This means that even when it is swimming along almost submerged, it can still breathe and see what is going on above the surface (*see p. 5*).

Hippos also enjoy a mud bath. Rolling in mud helps them to keep cool in very hot weather. During the day, hippos spend their time lying in mud holes (called "wallows") in the water, or on sandbanks.

Hippos are herbivorous, which means that they feed on plants and other vegetation, but do not eat meat. They pull up their food with their front teeth and grind it with their back teeth, called molars. They also have very big canine teeth, or tusks, on the lower jaw, which they may use to fight with if they find themselves cornered. These tusks are very heavy and may sometimes grow as long as 2 m. (6 ft.), although they are usually only half that length. The hippo has forty teeth altogether. When the animal feeds, it grinds

its teeth together constantly and wears them down. But the teeth (and tusks) do not wear away because they grow continuously.

Hippos usually come ashore to feed after dark. Each hippo makes its own trail or path from its watering place to its feeding ground. It uses the same trail every evening, finding its way home by following its own scent. These hippo trails can be seen clearly from the air (*right*).

These great beasts can eat as much as 136 kg. (300 lb.) of vegetation in the course of one feed! A hippo can work its way through a strip of land six miles long in a single night.

While they are feeding, hippos may wander as far as twenty miles from their lake or river. On the way, they may cause much damage along the river banks. They crash through cultivated areas, spoiling and eating young plants and flattening the soil with their heavy feet. If by chance they find fields of cultivated rice, sugar cane or corn stalks, they will eat as much as they can. When they have had enough, they may even pull up the corn stalks and take them back to their watering places. Then, when it is too hot for

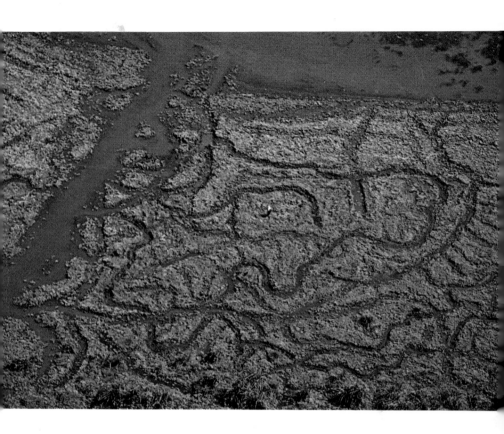

the hippo to move far in the midday sun, it can always find something left over from its midnight feast.

Hippos also eat the plants that grow on the surface of the river. The natives say that it is the purpose of these great beasts to keep the waterways and rivers clear for their boats.

You can imagine, however, that hippos are not popular when they cause havoc on cultivated land. This is partly why they were once hunted and killed in large numbers. The natives used to dig pits in the paths and tracks that the hippos followed each evening, and put a pointed stake in the middle. The animals were killed as they fell into the pits. They were also killed with guns, spears, and even bows and arrows. Often the hippos were not killed outright but only wounded, and would die a slow and painful death. This hippo has been wounded.

The flesh of the hippo, including its tongue, is a delicacy among African people. Its ivory tusks were once valuable. Hippo ivory was used to make false teeth, umbrella and stick handles, and fancy door knobs. These are other reasons why hippos were hunted in the past.

When catching several hippos, hunters armed with harpoons with lines attached would enter the water a little way from a herd, and swim quietly towards it. When they were near enough, the hunters all threw their weapons at the same time. A large wooden float was attached to each line. This

marked the position of the hippos if they submerged. Other hunters on the banks, also armed with harpoons and spears, then dragged the hippos on to the shore and killed them. To do this is now illegal, for the hippo is one of those animals protected by law; but a good deal of hunting and poaching probably still goes on in parts of Africa.

The only other enemy of the hippo, apart

from people, is the lion, which may occasionally spring on to the back of a hippo while it is feeding on land, and rake its hide with its claws. But this happens rarely.

A Common hippo was first brought to England and exhibited at London Zoo in 1850. Although in those days not very much was known about a hippo's diet, this animal lived until 1878. It also had an opportunity to mate with a female, which gave birth to a

baby hippo in 1871. Today, hippos in zoos are given hay, chaff, grass and roots, together with special vitamins and minerals to enrich their diet.

Hippos have attracted large crowds for a very long time. In 29 B.C., in the days of the ancient Romans, a hippo and five crocodiles were specially imported from Africa and shown together as an "act" in the Roman arena.

In the wild, a hippo will drink riverwater, but if it happens to be near the sea, it will also drink saltwater. The hippo appears to get on well with the water buffalo, and these two animals can often be seen drinking from the same water holes, or grazing together on the plains.

Although hippos may travel a long way when they are feeding, they are territorial animals. This means that they keep to their

own area of land or water during their lifetime. Like rhinos, they drop their dung in the same place day after day, and scatter it with extremely rapid movements of the tail. The hippo has been described as the nearest approach in nature to a mechanical manure-spreader! (*Right.*)

Hippos can usually be found in herds (or "schools") of between twenty and one hundred. It used to be thought at one time

that a hippo herd was led by the oldest male hippo, but we now know that a herd is ruled by the females, or cows. The hippo cows and their young live in a "crèche," or nursery, which is usually on a sandbank in the river or lake. There are separate small areas, called refuges, outside the central area. Each refuge is occupied by one adult male.

Strict rules of behavior have to be followed by all the members of the hippo herd. A female may pay a visit to a male in his refuge to mate outside the breeding season. He may then return her call, but he must be very polite. If one of the females gets up, the male must lie down; and he must not stand up again until she lies down! If he behaves badly, he may be attacked by all the full-grown females in the crèche! Here you can see the hippo's mating display.

A female is ready to mate when she is two or three years old. In the breeding season, she will move out of the crèche and choose a male. He cannot refuse to mate with her. Male hippos are protective. They become aggressive in the breeding season and will fight any rival males in the herd. With their massive tusks they can hurt each other

22

badly, although their wounds usually heal very quickly.

A baby hippo is born eight months or so after mating. This is a short time for such a large animal. On rare occasions a female will give birth to twins. The baby hippo is very heavy. It can weigh between 27 kg. (60 lb.) and 50 kg. (110 lb.) when it is born. That is about the weight of between ten and twenty newborn human babies! The baby hippo is nearly 1 m. (3 ft.) long and 0.5 m. (1.5 ft.) high, a quarter of its adult size.

Young hippos can be born in the water or on land. If a baby is born in the water, it will thrash about with its legs until it finds its way to the surface. Baby hippos which are born on land occasionally kick with their legs after birth as if they are treading water. Within five minutes of being born, baby hippos can walk, run and swim fairly well. They usually suckle from their mothers under the water, where it is safe.

Baby hippos are taught how to behave properly by their mothers. It is important for

them to learn to stay close to their mothers, because male hippos often get jealous of a new baby in the herd and may try and drive it out of the crèche. So, soon after it is born, the female takes her baby for walks, and teaches it to keep close to her side. It learns to run when she runs, stop when she stops, and turn when she turns. It also gets swimming lessons. In the water it must swim level with its mother's shoulder. Soon it will have learned to stay where its mother can defend it quickly from an aggressive male.

Hippo babies stay with their mothers for several years. If she has more than one, they all walk behind her in an orderly line, in order of age. The youngest walks behind the mother, and the eldest walks at the back. If a hippo baby is disobedient, the mother will punish it by rolling it over and over with her head, or even slashing it with her tusks. When the baby has learned its lesson, she will lick it and rub her head against it.

Baby hippos are usually more lively than their parents, and play in much the same

way as most baby animals do. They will rub their faces together, blow jets of water from their nostrils, and dive to the bottom of their river or lake. They come up regularly for air, as they are unable to stay under water for as long as adult animals. Babies can also be seen riding on their parents' heads and backs. They often do this in deep water, which they may find frightening when they are very small.

When male hippos grow big enough to leave the crèche, they have to find a refuge

outside the ring of adult males which lies
around the edge of the crèche. When the
younger hippo is old enough to mate with a
female, it has to fight for a place in one of
these "inner" refuges.

When a hippo "yawns" it does not mean
that it is feeling sleepy. The yawn is a
threatening gesture, and a challenge to a
fight. Fights between the males can be
fierce. Two hippos can be seen rearing up
out of the water, trying to cut each other
with their tusks. Each hippo tries to break

the front leg of its rival. With a broken leg a hippo is almost certain to die, because it will not be able to walk on land to feed and will soon starve to death.

In some areas, rivers may be blocked by a herd of hippos lying quietly in the water. A boat trying to travel down the river will then have to push its way through. These great animals will move slowly to one side with a great show of grunting and complaining. The noise a hippo makes, which sounds like a low "moo", can be heard for nearly a mile.

As they move, the hippos will shower water over the boat.

Hippos can be dangerous when they are disturbed in this way. People have lost their lives on lakes and rivers when an angry hippo has overturned their boat. These animals have been known to charge (*right*) at small steamers and make large enough holes in the sides to sink them.

An explorer and his team were once leading a herd of twenty cows across the River Nile, when they were attacked suddenly by several hippos. The hippos caught some of

the cows and dragged them under the water. The cows were never seen again.

Usually, however, hippos simply try to keep out of danger. One traveler in Africa described how he and his companion suddenly came to a river bank after struggling through a thick bush jungle. They saw a herd of at least twenty hippos on a stretch of white sand near the opposite bank. Their huge, bulky bodies made them look like a heap of black rocks. A water buffalo, which was standing on the far shore, was frightened at the sight of human beings and ran off. The hippos stood quite still and looked as if they were sleeping, but now and then they opened their eyes a little to look at the men. It was only when they heard the men speak that they all walked quickly one after the other into the river and swam to the middle. Here, it seems, they felt safe from any possible attack. Hippos often gather into a circle in the water for protection.

As the hippo lies on a sandbank or in the water, it attracts many different birds — such as weaver birds, cattle egrets, and even vultures. These birds sit on the backs of the hippos and look for ticks and flies on their

bodies. Hippos do not worry about this, because the ticks and flies irritate them. In the water, fish may clean a hippo's body by eating vegetable matter and mud sticking to the skin.

In warm, tropical West Africa, and parts of the Sudan, there is a miniature hippo called the Pygmy hippo (*right*), which is half the size of the Common hippo. It weighs approximately 360 kg. (800 lb.) The Pygmy hippo looks more like a wild boar then a true hippo, and differs in several ways from its larger relative.

The body of the Pygmy hippo is slimmer and more graceful than that of the Common hippo. Its teeth are smaller, and its eyes do not bulge out, but are small and very sharp. The hide of the Pygmy is brown or slategray, with a pink flush on the cheeks, throat and belly. The hide looks oily, because the pores in the skin secrete a clear, thick substance to keep the skin supple.

The behavior of the Pygmy hippo is also different from that of the Common hippo. It is much more at home on land, and only

enters the water to swim. If it is disturbed, the Pygmy hippo runs for cover in the undergrowth; it does not take to the water.

Moreover, Pygmy hippos are not found in herds. They stay in pairs or alone (although a traveler in Africa might be lucky enough to see a mother, father and baby grazing together.) This means that they are more difficult to find than the Common hippo. In fact, it was not until the beginning of the twentieth century that zoologists were sure that this shy animal really existed. The

Pygmy eats the same kinds of foods as the Common hippo. At night it sleeps in hollows in the banks of rivers.

In 1917, two Pygmy hippos were taken to the London Zoo, where they spent the winter in heated quarters. In the late spring they were moved out to Whipsnade Zoo, where they grazed in the fields and wallowed happily in the water.

More recently, we were lucky enough to be able to observe a young male Pygmy hippo at great length at our zoo in Ilfracombe. When he arrived, he would snort like a very angry boar, and used to open his mouth wide to show his teeth. He would bite anyone who upset him. After a little while, however, he became so tame that he would feed out of our hands.

We called him Percy. Percy liked potatoes, and he could always be persuaded to follow us if we offered him sweet rolls to eat. He particularly enjoyed apples and bananas — which he swallowed whole. We also found that he liked swimming in our small pond. When he came out of the water, however, his skin would dry up and look rather like a prune. So we would rub olive oil into his

skin. He loved this.

One day, Percy managed to push open the heavy wooden door of his pen. He then wandered down the drive towards a nearby house. Visitors scattered and ran in all directions, thinking that he was going to attack them. Percy stood still, watching the people quietly, and then started to walk across the

lawn. There was more panic.

Finally, I persuaded Percy to follow me back to his pen by tempting him with a large bunch of bananas. We put him back in and secured the door to stop him escaping again. Percy now lives at Paignton Zoo with a female who will, we hope, have a baby Pygmy hippo one of these days.

In the national parks of Africa, research into the behavior of hippos goes on all the time. In this picture, the men are tying the hippo's head to keep it still so that they can put a tag in its ear. This means that they can follow the movements of this hippo throughout its life.

The hippo in the other picture has been "darted." This means that a dart, containing a drug which will make it sleepy, has been shot into the hippo's side. The men can then look at the hippo closely, or treat it for

46

injury, without getting hurt themselves.

Zoologists want to find out as much as possible about all wild animals, so that they may take the action necessary to enable them to survive in today's world. The great

"leather-sided giant", as the Africans call the hippo, is a magnificent beast which deserves to live peacefully in its natural surroundings.

Glossary

AMPHIBIOUS An amphibious animal is able to live on land or in the water.

CRECHE A nursery group in which young animals live with adult females.

FOSSILIZED Changed into a fossil, which is the remains, impression or trace of an animal or plant found preserved in rock.

GAME RESERVE Large, supervised park where wild animals live in their natural surroundings, protected from hunters.

HARPOON A long, spear-like weapon which has a strong line attached to it so that an animal can be pulled in when it is hit.

HERBIVOROUS Feeding on plants and other vegetation, but not on meat or fish.

MAMMAL Warm blooded animal, the females of which suckle their young with milk.

PORES Tiny holes, especially the opening of a sweat gland in the skin. The pores in a hippo's skin secrete a substance which helps keep the animal waterproof.

REFUGE Small area outside the CRECHE. Each refuge is occupied by an adult male hippo.

SJAMBOK A whip which is made from the hide of hippos.

SUBMERGE To sink or dive under the water.

TERRITORIAL Keeping to a particular territory — an area in which an animal feeds and roams, and which it defends against others.

TICKS Insects which suck the blood of various animals for food. They may carry disease.

TUSK A long, pointed tooth on the lower jaw of the hippo. Other animals, such as elephants and walruses, also have tusks.

WALLOW A mud hole in which the hippo rolls to keep cool.

Further reading

Burton, Jane. *Animals of the African Year; The Ecology of East Africa*. New York: Holt, Rinehart and Winston, 1972.

Burton, Maurice and Burton, Robert, editors. *The New International Wildlife Encyclopedia*. 21 vols. Milwaukee: Purnell Reference Books, 1980.

Fisher, James, et. al. *Wildlife in Danger*. New York: Viking Press, 1969.

Hegner, Robert. *Parade of the Animal Kingdom*. New York: MacMillan Company, 1951.

Stanek, V. J. *Pictorial Encyclopedia of the Animal Kingdom*. New York: Crown Publishers, 1962.

Picture acknowledgements

Alan Hutchison Library, 7; Frank W. Lane, 26. All other pictures from Bruce Coleman Limited by the following photographers: Des Bartlett, 46; Jen & Des Bartlett, 34-5, 47; Jane Burton, 20-21; R.I.M. Campbell, endpapers, facing p.1, 2, 15, 18, back cover; Bruce Coleman, 9, 39, 42; Francisco Erize, 40; David Houston 25; M. P. Kahl, 5; Cyril Laubscher, 44-5; Lee Lyon, 4, 21, 23, 30; Norman Myers, 38, 48-9; G. D. Plage, 6, 11, 24; Hans Reinhard, 28, 32; N. M. Renh, 29; Leonard Lee Rue, 8; J. Pearson, 36; Norman Tomalin, 41; Simon Trevor, front cover, 1, 12-13, 16-17, 19, 27, 31, 33, 35.

Index